21-Day Hormone Reset

A Woman's Guide To Hormone Balance

Brittany Leckner

TABLE OF CONTENTS

Welcome to Your Hormone Reset Journey

Welcome to a sacred 21-day journey created for women who feel the quiet nudge that something within is asking to be rebalanced. This experience is designed to help you reconnect with your body's natural rhythms, restore vitality, and deepen your understanding of hormonal harmony through gentle, science-informed wellness practices.

This 21-Day Hormone Reset builds upon the foundation of the original 14-day reset, offering deeper guidance, daily rituals, and supportive lifestyle practices intended to help you tune back into your body—not override it. Rather than chasing quick fixes, this journey invites you to listen, learn, and respond with intention.

A Gentle Reset, not a Medical Prescription

Dear Beautiful Soul,

If you've been feeling tired, inflamed, emotionally sensitive, disconnected, or simply "not yourself," you are not broken—and you are not alone. Your body is always communicating. This reset is an invitation to slow down, reconnect, and understand those signals with compassion and clarity.

Over the next three weeks, you'll be guided through daily practices designed to support awareness of your endocrine system, reduce lifestyle stressors, and encourage harmony between mind, body, and spirit. This is not about control—it's about reconnection.

This program was created from years of functional wellness experience supporting women through hormonal transitions, metabolic stress, and periods of profound change. It blends intuitive wisdom with evidence-informed education to help you better understand why your body may be responding the way it is—and what supportive steps may be available to you.

Important Note on Scope & Empowerment

This program is educational in nature and is not intended to diagnose, treat, cure, or prevent any medical condition. It does not replace individualized medical care or advice from a licensed healthcare provider. Instead, it serves as a tool for self-awareness and empowerment—helping you gather insight, ask better questions, and make informed decisions about your health.

Whether the next step for you is implementing supportive practices at home, adjusting lifestyle rhythms, or seeking guidance from a qualified healthcare provider, this journey is designed to help you feel more confident and connected as you advocate for your own well-being.

You are the expert of your body. This reset simply helps you remember how to listen.

With reverence for your healing journey,

Brittany Leckner

How This Challenge Works

Daily Focus Areas

Each day features specific themes centered around food, movement, mindset, and hormone-supportive habits. These daily practices build upon each other to create a comprehensive reset experience. Guidance includes anti-inflammatory nutrition, appropriate exercise, stress management techniques, and self-care rituals specifically designed for women's hormone health.

Track Progress

Use the included checklist and symptom tracker to monitor the journey. Note changes in energy, mood, sleep quality, digestion, and other hormone-related markers throughout the 21 days. This data becomes invaluable for identifying personal hormone patterns and understanding which interventions make the biggest difference for unique biochemistry.

Community Support

Sharing experiences on social media or through email updates and questions connects women on similar journeys for motivation and accountability. Coaches monitor these channels and provide personalized guidance throughout the challenge experience. No one is alone in this transformation.

The original 14-day program was extended to 21 days to provide a more comprehensive experience. Research shows it takes approximately 21 days to establish new neural pathways for habits, making this reset the perfect foundation for lasting change. The additional week allows for deeper healing and more sustainable results.

Understanding Hormone Imbalance in Women 35+

Common Symptoms You May Be Experiencing:

Energy & Metabolism

- Persistent fatigue despite adequate sleep
- Stubborn weight gain especially around the abdomen
- Difficulty losing weight despite diet changes
- Afternoon energy crashes
- Feeling "wired but tired"

Mood & Cognition

- Unexpected mood swings
- Irritability and anxiety
- Depression or feelings of overwhelm
- Brain fog and difficulty concentrating
- Memory issues

Reproductive Health

- Irregular cycles and heavy periods
- Worsening PMS symptoms
- Perimenopausal changes
- Hot flashes and night sweats
- Fertility challenges

Sleep & Vitality

- Insomnia and disrupted sleep patterns
- Waking between 2-4 am

- Morning exhaustion
- Decreased interest in sex
- Reduced sense of vitality and zest for life

If several of these symptoms are present, this is a common experience. Hormone imbalance affects millions of women, particularly after age 35 when natural hormonal shifts accelerate. The good news is that many symptoms can be significantly improved through targeted lifestyle interventions, which this 21-day reset provides.

Key Hormones Targeted

This challenge addresses six of the most influential hormones for women in midlife. Understanding how these hormones function highlights the importance of each reset practice.

Estrogen

The primary female sex hormone regulating reproductive health and affecting mood, skin, bone density, and cognitive function. Imbalances can lead to mood swings, weight gain, and reproductive issues.

Progesterone

The calming hormone balancing estrogen and supporting sleep, mood stability, and thyroid function. Low levels can cause anxiety, sleep disturbances, and heavy periods.

Cortisol

The stress hormone that, when chronically elevated, disrupts all other hormones and contributes to inflammation, weight gain, and fatigue.

Insulin

The blood sugar regulator that, when imbalanced, leads to weight gain, cravings, energy crashes, and increased risk of chronic disease.

Thyroid Hormones

Metabolic controllers affecting energy, weight, temperature regulation, and overall vitality. Dysfunction can cause fatigue, weight changes, and cognitive issues.

Testosterone

Present in smaller amounts in women but crucial for libido, muscle tone, bone density, and mental clarity. Declining levels affect energy and vitality.

These hormones work together in delicate balance. When one becomes disrupted, it creates a domino effect impacting the entire system. This 21-day reset addresses all these hormones simultaneously through targeted nutrition, movement, stress management, and lifestyle practices.

The 21-Day Reset Framework: Your Roadmap to Balance

Anti-inflammatory Nutrition

Eliminate common inflammatory triggers while incorporating nutrient-dense whole foods that support detoxification pathways and hormone production. Focus on fiber-rich vegetables, quality proteins, and healthy fats that provide building blocks for hormone synthesis.

Blood Sugar Stabilization

Implement strategic meal timing and macronutrient balancing to prevent insulin spikes and crashes. This creates metabolic flexibility, reduces cortisol surges, and supports adrenal health, all crucial for hormone balance in midlife women.

Hormone-Sensitive Movement

Integrate resistance training and gentle movement patterns that stimulate muscle maintenance without triggering excessive cortisol. Exercise protocols are designed specifically for women's hormonal phases and changing needs after 35.

Gut & Liver Support

Focus on specific foods and practices that enhance detoxification pathways, particularly in the liver where hormones are processed. Support gut integrity to prevent reabsorption of estrogen metabolites and improve nutrient absorption.

Stress Reduction Protocols

Implement research-backed techniques to lower cortisol and activate the parasympathetic nervous system. These daily practices help break the cycle of stress-induced hormone disruption common in busy women over 35.

Each day of the 21-day journey incorporates elements from these five core areas, building progressively to create lasting change in hormonal health. The extended timeline allows for deeper implementation and more sustainable habit formation.

Your Daily Nutrition Guide: The Foundation of Hormone Health

Foods to Eliminate During the Reset:

Inflammatory Triggers

- Refined sugar and artificial sweeteners
- Conventional dairy products
- Gluten-containing grains
- Alcohol (even wine)
- Processed soy products
- Industrial seed oils (canola, vegetable, etc.)
- Ultra-processed foods and additives

Foods to Emphasize: Hormone Helpers

- Cruciferous vegetables (broccoli, cauliflower, Brussels sprouts)
- Healthy fats (avocado, olive oil, coconut)
- Omega-3 rich foods (wild-caught fish, walnuts, flax)
- Antioxidant-rich berries and colorful vegetables
- Clean proteins (pasture-raised eggs, grass-fed meats)
- Fiber-rich seeds (chia, flax, pumpkin)
- Bitter greens for liver support (dandelion, arugula)

Your Hormone-Balancing Plate:

For optimal hormone support, include these components in most meals:

Quality Protein (25-30%)

Pasture-raised eggs, wild-caught fish, grass-fed meats, or plant-based options like lentils and hemp seeds. Protein provides the amino acid building blocks for hormone production.

Colorful Vegetables (40-50%)

Aim for at least 2-3 cups per meal, emphasizing leafy greens and cruciferous vegetables that support estrogen metabolism and liver detoxification.

Healthy Fats (20-30%)

Avocados, olive oil, coconut oil, nuts, and seeds provide essential fatty acids required for hormone synthesis and cellular membrane health.

Flavor Enhancers

Anti-inflammatory herbs and spices like turmeric, ginger, cinnamon, and garlic not only add flavor but actively support hormone balance.

Sample Daily Menu for Hormone Balance

Morning

- Upon Waking: Warm lemon water with a pinch of sea salt to support adrenal function and hydration
- Breakfast: Green smoothie with collagen peptides, spinach, berries, avocado, and ground flaxseed (supports detoxification and provides essential fatty acids)

- Mid-Morning: Herbal tea (dandelion root or milk thistle) for liver support

Afternoon

- Lunch: Wild-caught salmon bowl with arugula, roasted sweet potato, fermented vegetables, and olive oil dressing (provides omega-3s, fiber, and prebiotics)
- Snack: Two Brazil nuts (selenium for thyroid) and celery with almond butter

Evening

- Dinner: Stir-fried broccoli and pasture-raised chicken with turmeric, ginger, coconut aminos, and cauliflower rice (offers cruciferous vegetables for estrogen metabolism and anti-inflammatory compounds)
- Evening: Calming chamomile or passionflower tea to support sleep

Proper hydration is essential for hormone balance. Throughout the day, aim for filtered water, mineral water, or herbal teas. A good goal is half your body weight in ounces of water daily.

Note on Timing:

Try to maintain at least 12 hours between dinner and breakfast the next day to support cellular repair and hormone regulation. For example, if dinner finishes at 7 PM, breakfast should be no earlier than 7 AM the next morning.

Week 1: Foundation - Strategic Movement for Hormone Balance

Days 1-3: Gentle Restoration

Begin with low-intensity movement that activates lymphatic drainage and increases circulation without stressing the adrenals:

- 20-30 minute nature walks, preferably in morning sunlight to regulate circadian rhythm and cortisol patterns
- Gentle yoga focusing on hip openers and spinal mobility (particularly cat-cow and child's pose)
- 5-10 minutes of rebounding on a mini-trampoline to stimulate lymphatic flow
- Deep breathing exercises: 4-7-8 breath pattern (4 count inhale, 7 count hold, 8 count exhale)

This phase prepares the body for more intensive movement while immediately supporting stress reduction.

Days 4-7: Foundation Building

Introduce targeted strength training to support metabolism and bone density:

- 20-minute full-body resistance sessions using bodyweight or light weights
- Focus on compound movements like modified squats, wall push-ups, and assisted lunges
- Pilates-inspired core work to strengthen the pelvic floor and deep abdominal muscles
- Continue daily walking, adding gentle inclines if available

Resistance training is particularly important for women over 35 as it helps maintain muscle mass which naturally declines with hormonal changes.

Week 2: Progressive - Advancing Your Movement Practice

Days 8-14: Metabolic Activation

Integrate more dynamic movement patterns while maintaining recovery focus:

- 2-3 resistance training sessions focusing on progressive overload (slightly increasing weight or repetitions)
- 1-2 sessions of low-impact interval training (30 seconds effort: 90 seconds recovery)
- Restorative yoga or targeted mobility work on recovery days
- Optional: foam rolling and fascial release to reduce tension patterns

This approach helps boost metabolism and improves insulin sensitivity without triggering excessive cortisol production.

Days 15-21: Integration & Personalization

During the final week, focus on discovering personal optimal movement patterns:

- Experiment with workout timing (morning vs. evening) to identify the hormonal sweet spot
- Test different movement styles to observe energy, mood, and recovery responses
- Modify intensity based on menstrual cycle phase or perimenopausal symptoms
- Develop a sustainable long-term movement plan

Exercise is a hormetic stressor, the right amount strengthens the system, while too much can worsen hormone imbalance. Listening to the body and adjusting intensity daily is essential. More is not always better for hormone balance.

Supplement & Self-Care Support System

Targeted Supplement Recommendations

Consult with a healthcare provider before beginning any supplement regimen, especially if there are existing health conditions or medications.

- **Magnesium Glycinate: 300-400mg daily**

- The "relaxation mineral" supporting over 300 enzymatic reactions in the body. Particularly helpful for sleep quality, muscle relaxation, and PMS symptoms. Many women are deficient due to soil depletion and stress.

- **Omega-3 Fatty Acids: 1-2g daily**

- Essential for reducing inflammation, supporting brain health, and providing building blocks for hormone production. Look for high-quality fish oil or algae-based supplements with at least 500mg combined EPA/DHA.

- **Adaptogenic Herbs**

- Ashwagandha (300-600mg) helps modulate cortisol levels and supports thyroid function. Rhodiola (200-400mg) improves stress resilience and energy. Holy basil tea supports adrenal health and blood sugar regulation.

Hormone-Specific Support

For estrogen dominance:	DIM (100-200mg) + Calcium-D-Glucarate (500mg)
For thyroid support:	Selenium (200mcg) + Zinc (15-30mg)
For progesterone support:	Vitamin B6 (50mg) + Vitex (160-240mg)
For insulin sensitivity:	Berberine (500mg) + Chromium (200mcg)
For cortisol balance:	Phosphatidylserine (300mg) + L-theanine (200mg)

Supplement needs vary based on unique hormone patterns, diet, lifestyle, and health history. The 21-day reset helps identify which supports provide the greatest benefit.

Daily Self-Care Rituals for Hormone Balance

Morning Rituals

- Dry Brushing: 3-5 minutes before showering to stimulate lymphatic drainage and support detoxification pathways

- Oil Pulling: 1 tablespoon of coconut oil swished for 5-10 minutes to reduce inflammatory burden
- Morning Sunlight: 10-15 minutes of direct sunlight exposure

to regulate circadian rhythm and cortisol patterns

- Gratitude Practice: 2-3 minutes writing down things to be grateful for to set a positive neurochemical tone

Midday Rituals

- Mindful Lunch: Eating away from screens, chewing thoroughly, and appreciating food
- Tension Release: 2-minute desk stretches or shoulder rolls to prevent stress accumulation
- Breathwork Break: 10 deep belly breaths to reset the nervous system
- Nature Connection: Even brief outdoor moments help reset cortisol patterns

Evening Rituals

- Castor Oil Packs: Applied over the liver area for 20-30 minutes to support detoxification (avoid during menstruation)
- Epsom Salt Baths: 2 cups in warm water with lavender essential oil for magnesium absorption and stress reduction
- Digital Sunset: Eliminating blue light exposure 2 hours before bed to support melatonin production
- Bedtime Gratitude: Reflecting on three positive moments from the day

These rituals may seem simple, but they create powerful neurological and hormonal shifts when practiced consistently. During the 21-day reset, adopting at least one ritual from each time period is encouraged. By the end of the program, these practices will feel like natural parts of the day rather than additional tasks.

Your Daily Tracker: The Key to Personalized Results

Research shows that women who track their hormone reset journey experience 68% better results than those who don't. Use this comprehensive tracker to identify patterns and celebrate progress.

21-Day Daily Tracker

Day	AM Routine	Nutrition	Movement	Hydration	Self-Care	Symptoms & Notes
1						
2						
3						
4						
5						
6						
7						
8						
9						
10						
11						
12						
13						
14						
15						
16						
17						
18						
19						
20						
21						

21-Day Daily Wellness Tracker

Day: _______________   **Date:** _______________

____

AM Routine

(check all that apply)

☐ Woke up without snoozing

☐ Morning light exposure

☐ Breathwork / prayer / meditation

☐ Supplements taken

☐ Cold or contrast shower

☐ Other: _______________________________________

____

Nutrition

(meals, timing, quality, notes)

Breakfast: _______________________________________

Lunch:

____

Dinner: _______________________________________

Snacks: _______________________________________

☐ Protein prioritized

☐ Anti-inflammatory foods

☐ No skipped meals

☐ Alcohol avoided / limited

Notes:

____

____

____

Movement

(type + duration)

☐ Walking

☐ Strength training

☐ Mobility / stretching

☐ Yoga / Pilates

☐ Other: _______________________________

Duration: ____________ minutes

Notes:

____

____

____

Hydration

(goal: ________ oz)

☐ Water upon waking

☐ Electrolytes

☐ Herbal tea

☐ Avoided sugary drinks

Total ounces consumed today: ___________

Notes:

____

____

____

Self-Care

(intentional nervous system support)

☐ Sleep routine followed

☐ Screen boundaries

☐ Sunlight / nature

☐ Sauna / bath / red light

☐ Journaling / reflection

Notes:

____

____

____

Symptoms & Notes

(track changes, wins, challenges)

Energy: ☐ Low ☐ Moderate ☐ High

Mood: ☐ Low ☐ Balanced ☐ Elevated

Digestion: ☐ Off ☐ Improving ☐ Great

Sleep quality: ☐ Poor ☐ Fair ☐ Restful

Additional Notes:

____

____

____

End-of-Day Reflection

One win today:

____

One thing to improve tomorrow:

____

Building Your Hormone-Safe Kitchen

Strategic Pantry Swaps

The foundation of hormone balance begins in the kitchen. These practical swaps eliminate common endocrine disruptors while introducing beneficial alternatives that support optimal hormone function.

Conventional Item	Hormone-Friendly Alternative	Benefit
Canola/Vegetable Oil	Extra Virgin Olive Oil, Avocado Oil	Reduces inflammatory omega-6 exposure
White Sugar	Monk Fruit, Stevia, Small amounts of Raw Honey	Stabilizes insulin response
Conventional Dairy	Coconut, Almond, or Cashew alternatives	Eliminates exogenous hormones
Soy Sauce	Coconut Aminos	Avoids phytoestrogens in processed soy
Plastic Food Storage	Glass or Stainless Steel Containers	Reduces xenoestrogen exposure
Non-stick Cookware	Cast Iron, Stainless Steel, Ceramic	Eliminates PFAS chemicals
Conventional Produce	Organic (especially for the "Dirty Dozen")	Reduces pesticide exposure
Processed Snacks	Raw Nuts, Seed Crackers, Fresh Fruit	Provides nutrient density

Making these switches gradually over the 21 days helps create a kitchen environment that supports rather than disrupts hormonal health. Start with the swaps that feel most manageable and build from there.

Hormone-Supporting Staples to Stock

Dry Goods

- Gluten-free grains: quinoa, millet, buckwheat
- Legumes: lentils, chickpeas, black beans
- Seeds: flax, chia, pumpkin, hemp, sesame
- Nuts: walnuts, Brazil nuts, almonds, cashews
- Seaweeds: dulse, nori, wakame (for iodine)
- Teas: spearmint, dandelion root, milk thistle

Refrigerator Staples

- Dark leafy greens: kale, spinach, arugula, collards
- Cruciferous vegetables: broccoli, cauliflower, Brussels sprouts
- Fermented foods: sauerkraut, kimchi, kefir
- Quality proteins: pasture-raised eggs, wild-caught fish

- Berries: blueberries, strawberries, raspberries
- Fresh herbs: cilantro, parsley, rosemary, basil

Cooking Essentials

- Anti-inflammatory spices: turmeric, ginger, cinnamon
- Quality oils: extra virgin olive oil, avocado oil, coconut oil
- Apple cider vinegar (with "the mother")
- Bone broth or vegetable broth (homemade or clean-ingredient store versions)

During the 21-day reset, focus on whole, single-ingredient foods as much as possible. These staples provide the nutrient density needed to support hormone production, detoxification, and cellular repair.

Mindset & Emotional Healing: The Missing Link

Hormone balance isn't just physical, thoughts, beliefs, and emotional patterns directly impact the endocrine system through neuroendocrine pathways. Use these journal prompts to address the mind-body connection.

Intention Setting

- What specifically made you start this hormone reset challenge? Go beyond surface-level symptoms to explore deeper motivations.
- How would life change if hormones were perfectly balanced? Visualize this in detail, engaging all senses.
- What beliefs are held about the body's ability to heal? Are these empowering or limiting?

Body Connection

- How does the body feel today on a scale of 1-10? Where is there tension, discomfort, or ease?
- What messages might symptoms be trying to communicate? If fatigue/anxiety/pain could speak, what would it say?
- When was the last time truly vibrant and energetic feelings were

experienced? What elements from that time could be reintegrated now?

Nutrition Awareness

- Which foods create feelings of energy and which leave feeling depleted? Track these patterns over 21 days.
- What is the emotional relationship with food? Is it used for comfort, control, pleasure, or fuel?
- How has cultural background shaped food choices? Which traditions support hormone health?

Limiting Beliefs

- What stories are told about aging and hormonal changes? Are these based on fact or fear?
- Which limiting beliefs are ready to be released? (e.g., "Hormone problems are inevitable" or "I'll never feel good again")
- What new empowering beliefs would better serve the healing journey?

Set aside 10-15 minutes daily to reflect on these prompts in a journal. This practice creates awareness of emotional patterns that may affect hormonal health and opens the door to profound healing.

Emotional Healing Practices

Stress Pattern Identification

Research shows chronic stress is a primary disruptor of hormone balance for women over 35. Use a journal to identify personal stress triggers and patterns.

Common triggers include:

- Perfectionism and people-pleasing tendencies

- Caretaking responsibilities without adequate support
- Career pressure and workplace dynamics
- Financial concerns or insecurity
- Relationship challenges or conflict avoidance
- Unprocessed grief or past trauma

Emotional Release Techniques

Once patterns are identified, implement these evidence-based techniques:

- **EFT Tapping**
- A form of psychological acupressure that reduces cortisol by 24% in clinical studies. Involves tapping on specific meridian points while addressing emotional issues.

- **Heart-Focused Breathing**
- Developed by HeartMath Institute to regulate heart rate variability. Place a hand over the heart and breathe slowly while focusing on feelings of appreciation.

- **Expressive Writing**
- Spending 15-20 minutes writing about emotional experiences without editing or censoring. This process helps process emotions that may be stored in the body.

- **Self-Compassion Practice**
- Speaking to oneself with the kindness offered to a friend. Research shows self-compassion lowers cortisol and improves hormone balance.

During weeks 2 and 3 of the reset, specific emotional healing practices tailored to common hormone imbalance patterns will be introduced.

The Hormone - Sleep Connection: Optimizing Your Circadian Rhythm

Sleep is perhaps the most critical yet overlooked component of hormone balance. During sleep, the body conducts essential repair processes, balances hormone levels, and clears metabolic waste. For women over 35, sleep disruption correlates directly with worsening hormone symptoms.

The Science of Hormonal Sleep Cycles

The sleep-wake cycle is regulated by the complex interplay of several hormones:

Cortisol

Should naturally peak in early morning to help wake up, then gradually decline throughout the day, reaching its lowest point around midnight.

Melatonin

Begins rising about 2 hours before bedtime when light levels decrease, signaling the body that it's time to prepare for sleep.

Growth Hormone

Released primarily during deep sleep phases, supporting tissue repair and metabolic functions.

Insulin

Becomes more sensitive during proper sleep cycles, helping to maintain stable blood sugar overnight.

When these cycles are disrupted, it creates a cascade of hormone imbalances affecting everything from thyroid function to estrogen metabolism.

Common Sleep Disruptors After 35

Several factors become more prevalent as women enter perimenopause and beyond:

Hormonal Disruptions

- Night Sweats: Fluctuating estrogen can trigger thermoregulation issues
- Cortisol Dysregulation: Stress and adrenal fatigue can flip cortisol patterns, causing nighttime alertness
- Thyroid Imbalance: Can cause both insomnia and excessive fatigue

Physiological Factors

- Blood Sugar Instability: Midnight waking between 2-4 am often signals a blood sugar drop
- Magnesium Deficiency: Affects GABA production and muscle relaxation
- Digestive Issues: Gut inflammation can increase cortisol and disrupt sleep

Environmental Influences

- Digital Disruption: Blue light exposure suppresses melatonin production
- Irregular Sleep Schedule: Disrupts natural hormone timing
- Bedroom Environment: Temperature, noise, and light affect sleep quality

Your Reset Sleep Protocol

Implement these evidence-based strategies during the 21-day reset:

- Consistent Schedule: Go to bed and wake at the same times daily, even on weekends
- Morning Sunlight: Get 10-15 minutes of direct morning sunlight to anchor the circadian rhythm
- Evening Wind-Down: Create a 30-minute pre-sleep ritual free from screens and stimulation

- Bedroom Optimization: Keep the sleeping environment cool (65-68°F), completely dark, and quiet
- Blood Sugar Stabilization: Consider a small protein-fat snack before bed if waking at night
- Supplement Support: Magnesium glycinate (300-400mg) and L-theanine (200mg) can support relaxation

Many women report significant improvements in sleep quality by Day 5-7 of the reset as inflammation decreases and hormones begin rebalancing.

Understanding Your Unique Hormone Type

While all women share the same hormones, the way they interact creates distinctive patterns. Identifying the primary hormone imbalance type helps customize the approach for optimal results.

Estrogen Dominant

Common Signs: Heavy periods, breast tenderness, mood swings, weight gain in hips/thighs, fibroids, endometriosis

Reset Focus: Support liver detoxification, increase fiber intake, reduce environmental estrogens, emphasize cruciferous vegetables

Key Supplements: DIM, calcium-d-glucarate, B vitamins, magnesium

Thyroid Imbalanced

Common Signs: Fatigue, cold intolerance, constipation, dry skin, weight gain despite diet changes, hair thinning, brain fog

Reset Focus: Support gut health, reduce inflammatory triggers, moderate exercise, iodine-rich foods

Key Supplements: Selenium, zinc, iron (if deficient), vitamin D, adaptogenic herbs

Insulin Resistant

Common Signs: Sugar cravings, fatigue after meals, belly fat accumulation, skin tags, PCOS symptoms, afternoon energy crashes

Reset Focus: Blood sugar balancing, protein at each meal, intermittent fasting window, strategic movement

Key Supplements: Berberine, chromium, magnesium, alpha-lipoic acid, inositol

Cortisol Dominant

Common Signs: Wired but tired, sleep disruption, anxiety, afternoon slumps, salt cravings, mild depression

Reset Focus: Stress reduction protocols, gentle movement, blood sugar stability, circadian rhythm reset

Key Supplements: Adaptogenic herbs, magnesium, B vitamins, vitamin C, phosphatidylserine

During the 21-day reset, pay close attention to which symptoms improve most dramatically and which foods or practices provide the greatest relief. This self-discovery process often reveals the primary hormone pattern.

Recommended Hormone Testing

For a more precise assessment of hormone health, consider these testing options after completing the initial reset:

DUTCH Complete

The gold standard for comprehensive hormone testing, measuring metabolites of estrogen, progesterone, testosterone, cortisol, and more. This dried urine test provides detailed insights into hormone production and metabolism.

Full Thyroid Panel

Including TSH, Free T3, Free T4, Reverse T3, and thyroid antibodies. Standard thyroid tests often miss subclinical imbalances that can significantly impact energy, metabolism, and mood.

Fasting Insulin and Glucose

To assess insulin resistance more accurately than standard blood sugar tests. These markers can identify metabolic issues years before they become clinical problems.

Micronutrient Testing

To identify specific deficiencies affecting hormone production. Many hormone imbalances are driven by nutritional gaps that can be effectively addressed with targeted supplementation.

Complete Blood Count and Metabolic Panel

These basic tests provide important information about overall health, inflammation levels, and organ function that impact hormone balance.

Testosterone Assessment

It is important that testosterone levels be measured just as any other hormone. Outdated myths should not deter checking testosterone levels or seeking professional advice.

Working with a functional medicine practitioner or women's health specialist can help interpret these results and develop a long-term hormone balancing strategy based on unique biochemistry. If unsure where to start, Brittany Leckner offers consultations to guide toward the right professionals and testing.

Navigating Common Challenges During the Reset

Understanding Detox Symptoms

As the body begins releasing stored toxins and adjusting to new hormone-supporting habits, temporary discomfort may be experienced. These symptoms typically peak around days 3-5 and resolve by day 7.

Common Detox Reactions

- Headaches: Often related to caffeine withdrawal or toxin release
- Fatigue: The body is diverting energy to healing processes
- Digestive Changes: New fiber intake and microbiome shifts
- Skin Breakouts: Temporary as toxins exit through skin
- Mood Fluctuations: Hormones rebalancing and blood sugar stabilizing
- Cravings: Brain chemistry adjusting to reduced sugar/processed foods

Supportive Strategies:

- Hydration: Increase water intake to support elimination (aim for half body weight in ounces)
- Epsom Salt Baths: Draw toxins out through the skin while absorbing magnesium
- Gentle Movement: Stimulates lymphatic flow without adding stress

- Rest: Honor the body's need for additional sleep during this transition
- Digestive Support: Digestive enzymes or bitters before meals if experiencing bloating

Important Reminder: Detox symptoms are actually a positive sign that the body is releasing stored toxins and beginning to heal. However, if symptoms are severe or persist beyond one week, consult with a healthcare provider.

Social Situations & Dining Out

Maintaining the reset doesn't mean isolating oneself. Use these strategies for navigating social events while supporting hormone health.

Restaurant Strategies:

- Review menus online beforehand to identify hormone-friendly options
- Request simple modifications (steamed instead of fried, dressing on the side)
- Focus on clean proteins and vegetables, avoiding sauces with hidden sugar or seed oils
- Consider eating a small protein snack before events with limited options
- Bring herbal tea bags to enjoy after dinner instead of dessert
- Choose sparkling water with lime instead of alcohol

Social Pressure Solutions:

- Prepare a simple explanation of health goals without oversharing
- Offer to bring a dish to gatherings that supports the reset
- Shift focus from food to connection by suggesting activity-based gatherings
- Practice assertive but kind boundary-setting with food pushers

- Remember that the health journey is personal and doesn't require others' approval

The 21-day timeframe is specifically designed to be sustainable while still providing meaningful results. Remember that this is a reset, not a permanent restriction, focus on what is being gained rather than what is temporarily modified.

The Hormone-Gut Connection: Healing Your Microbiome

Research increasingly shows that gut health is intimately connected to hormone balance. The intestinal microbiome influences estrogen metabolism, cortisol regulation, and even thyroid hormone conversion.

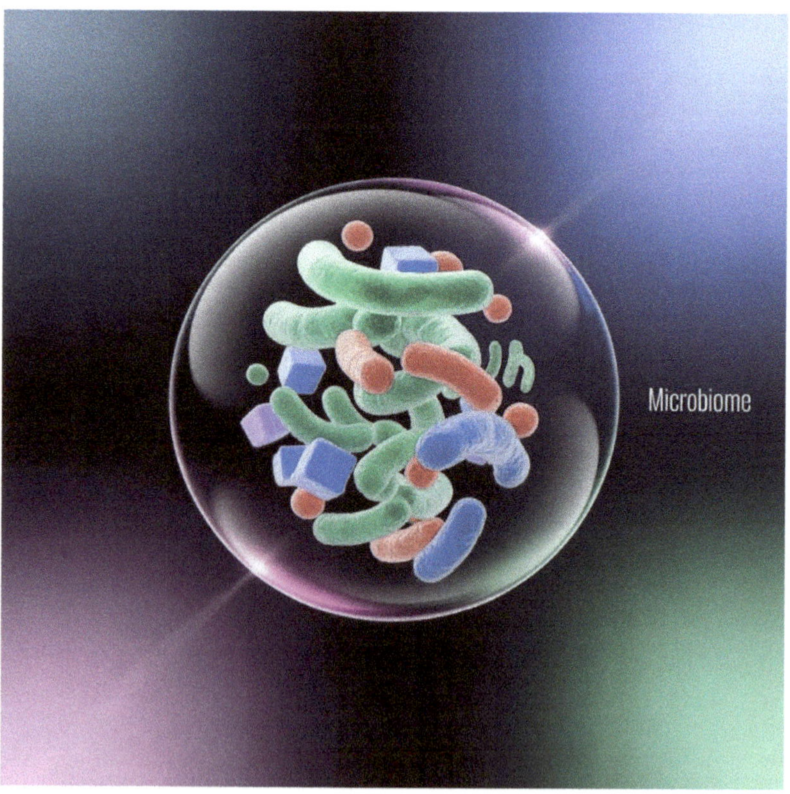

Your Estrobolome

A specialized collection of gut bacteria that metabolize and recycle estrogen. When imbalanced, these bacteria can either reactivate estrogen that should be eliminated (contributing to estrogen dominance) or fail to produce beneficial estrogen metabolites. Supporting these bacteria is crucial for healthy estrogen balance.

Gut Permeability

Leaky gut syndrome allows inflammatory compounds to enter circulation, triggering immune responses that interfere with hormone receptors. These inflammatory cytokines can block hormone signaling at the cellular level, creating a situation where adequate hormones exist but receptor response is poor.

T4 to T3 Conversion

Approximately 20% of thyroid hormone conversion happens in the gut. Intestinal inflammation and dysbiosis can significantly impair this process, leading to hypothyroid symptoms even when blood tests appear normal.

Gut-Brain Axis

The enteric nervous system (gut) communicates directly with the brain via the vagus nerve, influencing neurotransmitter production and HPA axis function. This bidirectional communication affects stress hormone regulation, mood stability, and sleep quality.

During weeks 2 and 3 of the reset, specific gut healing protocols will be introduced to optimize the microbiome and support hormone balance.

Microbiome-Supporting Reset Strategies

Foods to Emphasize:

- Prebiotic Fibers: Jerusalem artichokes, garlic, onions, leeks, asparagus, and green bananas feed beneficial bacteria

- Fermented Foods: Sauerkraut, kimchi, and coconut yogurt provide living probiotic strains
- Polyphenol-Rich Foods: Berries, green tea, olive oil, and dark chocolate support microbiome diversity
- Bitter Greens: Dandelion, arugula, and endive stimulate digestive enzyme production
- Omega-3 Fats: Wild-caught fish and flaxseeds reduce intestinal inflammation

Gut-Healing Practices:

- Intermittent Fasting: A 12-14 hour overnight fast supports intestinal cell regeneration
- Mindful Eating: Thoroughly chewing and eating without distraction improves digestion
- Bone Broth: Contains glycine, glutamine, and collagen that support gut lining repair
- Stress Management: Activating parasympathetic "rest and digest" mode before meals
- Hydration Between Meals: Supports mucus membrane integrity without diluting digestive enzymes

During the 21-day reset, aim to include at least one fermented food daily and gradually increase prebiotic fiber intake. This approach helps rebuild a healthy microbiome without triggering excessive die-off symptoms that can occur with more aggressive protocols.

Age-Specific Hormone Considerations

While the core principles of hormone balance apply to all women over 35, specific concerns emerge during different life stages. Understanding the unique position on the hormonal timeline helps prioritize the most relevant aspects of the reset.

Mid-30s to Early 40s

- Primary Changes: Subtle progesterone decline, ovulation becomes less regular
- Common Symptoms: PMS intensifies, sleep disruption begins, stress resilience decreases
- Reset Focus: Progesterone support, stress management, blood sugar stability
- Key Practices: Seed cycling, vitamin C supplementation, consistent exercise routine
- Success Markers: Improved menstrual regularity, reduced PMS, stable energy

Mid-40s to Early 50s (Perimenopause)

- Primary Changes: Significant estrogen fluctuations, progesterone decline, irregular cycles
- Common Symptoms: Hot flashes, mood swings, brain fog, weight redistribution, vaginal dryness
- Reset Focus: Adrenal support, phytoestrogen moderation, liver detoxification
- Key Practices: Adaptogenic herbs, omega-3 supplementation, resistance training
- Success Markers: Reduced hot flashes, improved emotional stability, better sleep

Post-Menopause (1+ Years After Last Period)

- Primary Changes: Consistently low estrogen and progesterone, adrenal hormones become primary source
- Common Symptoms: Bone density concerns, metabolic slowing, cardiovascular changes
- Reset Focus: Metabolism support, bone health, cardiovascular protection
- Key Practices: Strength training, vitamin K2 and D3 supplementation, nitric oxide production

- Success Markers: Stable weight, maintained muscle mass, cardiovascular health

During the 21-day reset, specific guidance tailored to each age group and hormonal stage is provided.

Customizing the Reset by Age

For Women in Their 30s-Early 40s:

Focus on preventative practices that lay the foundation for long-term hormone health:

- Emphasize detoxification support through cruciferous vegetables and liver-supporting herbs
- Prioritize stress management to preserve adrenal function before perimenopause begins
- Build muscle mass now to support metabolism during later transitions
- Address gut health and inflammation early to prevent accelerated hormone decline
- Consider seed cycling to support natural hormone rhythms (flax/pumpkin seeds first half of cycle, sesame/sunflower second half)

For Women in Perimenopause and Beyond:

Focus on adaptive strategies that support the body's changing needs:

- Emphasize phytoestrogens like flaxseed and fermented soy in moderation
- Increase focus on adrenal support as ovarian hormone production declines
- Prioritize bone-building through targeted nutrition and resistance exercise
- Support cognitive function with omega-3 fatty acids and brain-nourishing foods
- Consider targeted supplementation for specific symptoms (black cohosh for hot flashes, maca for libido, etc.)

The 21-day reset provides core strategies that benefit all women, but special attention is encouraged toward recommendations that align with the current life stage for optimal results.

The Importance of Cyclical Living After the Reset

Even after menopause, women's bodies continue to respond to cyclical rhythms. Aligning lifestyle with these natural cycles, both internal and external, creates sustainable hormone balance long after the 21-day reset concludes.

Honoring Hormonal Rhythms:

For Menstruating Women:

Research shows that women perform differently throughout their menstrual cycle due to hormonal fluctuations. After the reset, continue aligning activities with cycle phases:

Follicular Phase (Days 1-14)

Rising estrogen supports creativity, learning, and starting new projects. This is an optimal time for:

- High-intensity workouts and strength training
- Creative brainstorming and problem-solving
- Social activities and networking
- Lighter, more energizing foods

Luteal Phase (Days 15-28)

Progesterone rises, then both hormones fall. During this time, focus on:

- Lower-intensity movement and restorative exercise
- Detail-oriented tasks and completion of projects
- Self-care and introspection
- Warming, grounding foods with additional calories

For Post-Menopausal Women:

Without a menstrual cycle, align with natural circadian and seasonal rhythms:

Daily Cycles

- Morning (6am-10am): Highest cortisol, best for exercise and analytical tasks

- Midday (10am-2pm): Peak alertness, ideal for decision-making and meetings
- Afternoon (2pm-6pm): Slight energy dip, good for creative work
- Evening (6pm-10pm): Rising melatonin, time to wind down activities

Seasonal Cycles

- Spring: Focus on liver support and gentle detoxification
- Summer: Higher activity levels and social connection
- Fall: Immune system strengthening and boundary setting
- Winter: Increased rest, reflection, and deeper nourishment

Honoring these natural rhythms reduces stress on adrenal glands, which become the primary hormone producers after menopause.

Week 3: Integration and Personalization

The final week of the reset focuses on helping create a sustainable plan for continued hormone balance after the 21 days are complete.

Days 15-16: Pattern Recognition

Review the symptom tracker and identify clear patterns between specific foods, activities, or stressors and hormone symptoms. This data becomes a personalized hormone blueprint.

Days 17-18: Experimentation

Begin carefully testing variations in the protocol to determine personal thresholds and optimal approaches. This might include adjusting meal timing, workout intensity, or sleep schedule.

Days 19-20: Customization

Based on these discoveries, create a personalized hormone balancing plan that incorporates the reset elements that provided the greatest benefit for the unique body.

Day 21: Future Planning

Establish a long-term hormone health strategy with specific, achievable action steps and contingency plans for challenging situations like travel, illness, or high-stress periods.

This personalization phase distinguishes this 21-day reset from shorter programs. The additional week allows moving beyond the initial detoxification and stabilization phases into true hormonal integration and personalized understanding.

Final Reflection & Maintenance Strategies

As the 21-day reset concludes, take time to reflect on the experience and plan for sustainable hormone health moving forward.

Evaluating Results:

Review daily tracker and journal entries to identify key patterns:

- Symptom Improvement
- Most women experience at least a 70% reduction in primary hormone-related symptoms within 21 days of following the complete protocol.
- Days for Habit Formation
- Research shows it takes approximately 21 days to begin establishing new neural pathways for habits, making this reset the perfect foundation for lasting change.
- Key Insights
- Identify at least 3 major revelations about unique hormone patterns, sensitivities, and most effective support strategies.

Questions for Reflection:

1. Which specific foods or practices provided the most noticeable benefits?

2. What unexpected changes were observed beyond initial symptoms?

3. Which aspects of the reset were most challenging, and how might these be addressed moving forward?

4. What hormone type is believed to be the primary pattern based on responses?

5. Which aspects of the reset feel most motivating to continue long-term?

Creating a Maintenance Plan

Use these guidelines to develop a sustainable approach after the reset:

The 80/20 Approach

Most women find optimal balance by following reset principles 80% of the time while allowing flexibility for 20% of meals and activities. This prevents perfectionism while maintaining results.

Food Reintroduction Protocol

1. Select ONE eliminated food to reintroduce at a time

2. Consume a normal portion for 1-2 meals

3. Wait 72 hours while monitoring for reactions (energy, digestion, skin, mood)

4. Record responses in a journal before trying the next food

5. Permanently limit or avoid foods that trigger significant symptoms

Core Habits to Maintain

- Morning hydration and protein-rich breakfast
- Regular movement appropriate for hormonal phase
- Consistent sleep-wake cycle
- Daily stress management practice (even 5-10 minutes)
- Weekly meal preparation
- Continued avoidance of personal trigger foods
- Regular check-ins with symptom tracker
- Seasonal mini-resets (3-5 days) for ongoing support

Remember that hormone balance is not about perfection, it's about creating a loving relationship with the body and honoring its wisdom at every stage of life. Small, consistent actions create powerful cumulative effects on hormonal health.

Men's Testosterone & Vitality Boost

A male-focused hormone optimization program addressing declining testosterone, energy issues, and metabolic health. Features strength training protocols, nutrient timing strategies, and targeted supplements for male hormone support.

21-Day Metabolic Ignition Program

Designed for stubborn weight loss resistance, this program focuses on metabolic flexibility, insulin sensitivity, and fat adaptation. Includes carb-cycling meal plans, HIIT workout sequences, and lifestyle practices to optimize metabolic function.

Additional Challenge Kits

"No Spend" Budget Challenge

Address financial wellness with this guided 30-day program to reset spending habits, establish healthy money routines, and reduce financial stress, a significant contributor to hormone imbalance. Includes tracking tools, mindset work, and practical saving strategies.

Home Detox: Clean Living Starter Kit

Eliminate endocrine-disrupting chemicals from the environment with this room-by-room guide to creating a hormone-safe home. Includes recipes for non-toxic cleaning products, personal care alternatives, and a curated shopping guide for clean household items.

Beginner Gym Babe Muscle Activation

Perfect for women new to strength training or returning after a break, this 4-week program focuses on proper form, progressive overload, and confidence building. Includes instructional videos, gym anxiety management techniques, and hormone-optimizing workout scheduling.

14-Day Home Detox Kit

A practical guide to identifying and removing everyday toxins that disrupt hormones, inflame your body, and exhaust your energy. Designed for busy health-conscious families, this challenge equips you with simple daily steps, educational insights, and powerful tools to clean up your space and reclaim your health.

Each specialized kit was developed based on clinical experience and the latest research. Health is addressed holistically, recognizing that hormone balance is influenced by multiple factors including nutrition, movement, stress, environment, and mindset.

Share Your Journey & Stay Connected

Join Thriving Community

The hormone reset journey doesn't end here, it's just the beginning of a supported path to vibrant health. Connect with others who understand this experience.

Social Media

You can find us and like the pages at:

- Facebook: Brittany Leckner
- TikTok: @justaroundthiscorner
- Instagram: @leckner_brittany, @solutions_for_internal_success

Next Steps:

1. Complete final reflection in a journal, documenting all experienced changes

2. Decide which program best fits continuing needs based on primary hormone patterns

3. Share experience with someone who might benefit from this reset

4. Schedule a follow-up assessment in 3 months to track continued progress

Contact Information:

💼 Business Inquiries, clinical concerns and for further support and referrals: info@sacredsolutionsconsulting.com

The Role of Testosterone in Women's Health

Often overlooked in women's hormone discussions, testosterone plays a vital role in female health and vitality. This powerful hormone affects far more than just libido.

Why Testosterone Matters for Women:

- Muscle Maintenance: Supports lean muscle mass, essential for metabolism and longevity
- Bone Density: Works with estrogen to maintain strong bones and prevent osteoporosis
- Cognitive Function: Influences focus, mental clarity, and memory
- Energy Levels: Contributes to overall vitality and resilience
- Mood Regulation: Helps prevent depression and anxiety
- Sexual Function: Affects desire, arousal, and satisfaction

Signs of Low Testosterone in Women

- Persistent fatigue despite adequate rest
- Decreased muscle tone despite regular exercise
- Reduced motivation and drive
- Brain fog and difficulty concentrating
- Low libido and diminished sexual satisfaction
- Mood changes including irritability or depression

Many women attribute these symptoms solely to estrogen or progesterone imbalances, missing the crucial testosterone component of the hormone puzzle.

Expert Insight:

"Don't let outdated myths deter you from checking testosterone levels or seeking professional advice. For many women, addressing testosterone balance can be the missing piece in their hormone health puzzle.", Brittany Leckner, Hormone Specialist

Supporting Healthy Testosterone Levels Naturally

Nutrition Strategies

- Include healthy fats daily (avocados, olive oil, nuts, seeds)
- Ensure adequate protein intake (0.8-1g per pound of lean body mass)
- Incorporate zinc-rich foods (oysters, pumpkin seeds, grass-fed beef)
- Include cholesterol from healthy sources (eggs, grass-fed meats) as it's the precursor to all hormones
- Optimize vitamin D levels through sun exposure and supplementation if needed

Lifestyle Approaches

- Prioritize resistance training 2-3 times weekly to stimulate natural testosterone production
- Ensure adequate sleep (7-9 hours) as most testosterone is produced during deep sleep
- Manage stress effectively to prevent cortisol from depleting testosterone
- Maintain a healthy body fat percentage (neither too high nor too low)
- Limit alcohol consumption as it can suppress testosterone production

Testing Recommendations

- Request a complete hormone panel that includes total and free testosterone
- Test DHEA-S levels (a testosterone precursor)
- Check sex hormone binding globulin (SHBG) which affects testosterone availability
- Consider Dutch testing for a comprehensive view of hormone metabolism
- Track symptoms alongside lab results for a complete picture
- During the 21-day hormone reset, many practices, particularly resistance training, quality sleep, stress management, and balanced nutrition, naturally support healthy testosterone production. Continued attention to these factors after the reset helps maintain optimal levels.

Understanding Unique Hormone Patterns

One of the most valuable outcomes of the 21-day reset is gaining insight into personal hormone patterns. By tracking symptoms and responses throughout the program, it becomes easier to recognize how unique biochemistry responds to different inputs.

Cyclical Patterns

Notice which symptoms appear at specific times in the menstrual cycle or at regular intervals. These patterns often reveal which hormones are primarily imbalanced.

Food Responses

Track how different foods affect energy, mood, digestion, and sleep. Specific food sensitivities that disrupt hormone balance may be discovered.

Stress Triggers

Identify which stressors have the strongest impact on hormonal symptoms. This awareness allows implementation of targeted stress management strategies.

Sleep Influences

Observe how sleep quality affects hormone-related symptoms and which factors most impact sleep. This helps prioritize sleep hygiene practices.

Movement Effects

Notice how different types and intensities of exercise affect energy, mood, and symptoms. This helps create a personalized movement plan.

Environmental Factors

Recognize how environmental elements like light exposure, temperature, and toxins influence hormone balance and overall wellbeing.

Understanding these patterns empowers informed decisions about health long after the 21-day reset is complete. The body is constantly communicating, the reset helps to learn its unique language.

Adapting the Reset for Different Lifestyles

For the Busy Professional

Time constraints are one of the biggest challenges to implementing hormone-supportive habits. Here's how to make the reset work with a demanding schedule:

- Meal Prep Efficiency: Dedicate 2-3 hours on weekends to batch-cook proteins and roast vegetables for quick meal assembly
- Micro-Workouts: Break exercise into 10-minute segments throughout the day (morning, lunch break, evening)
- Desk-Friendly Practices: Incorporate deep breathing, desk stretches, and stress-reduction techniques during work hours
- Travel Strategies: Pack hormone-supporting supplements, portable snacks, and a travel workout plan
- Digital Boundaries: Create technology curfews to support melatonin production and stress reduction

For Parents and Caregivers

Balancing health needs with caring for others requires strategic approaches:

- Family-Friendly Reset Meals: Adapt reset recipes to be enjoyed by the whole family while meeting specific needs
- Include Children in Movement: Create playful movement activities that double as exercise
- Tag-Team Support: Coordinate with partners, family members, or friends to create space for self-care
- Multi-Tasking Self-Care: Practice meditation or deep breathing while supervising children's activities
- Modeling Health: Use this as an opportunity to teach children about listening to their bodies

Remember that imperfect implementation is still beneficial. Focus on consistency rather than perfection, and celebrate small wins along the hormone balance journey.

Understanding the Science: How the Reset Creates Hormonal Change

The 21-Day Hormone Reset isn't just a collection of healthy habits, it's a strategically designed program based on the physiological mechanisms of hormone regulation. Understanding these mechanisms helps appreciate why each component of the reset is important.

- **Cellular Response**
- Improved receptor sensitivity and mitochondrial function

- **Metabolic Pathways**
- Enhanced hormone production, conversion, and detoxification

- **Organ Systems**
- Optimized function of adrenals, ovaries, thyroid, liver, and gut

- **Whole-Body Integration**
- Synchronized communication between endocrine, nervous, and immune systems

- **Lifestyle Practices**
- Nutrition, movement, sleep, stress management, and environmental factors that support all levels

During the first week of the reset, the focus is primarily on reducing inflammatory triggers and supporting detoxification pathways. By week two, the body begins enhancing hormone production and receptor sensitivity. By week three, improved communication between endocrine, nervous, and immune systems occurs.

This progressive approach allows the body to heal systematically rather than attempting to address all systems simultaneously, which can overwhelm adaptive capacity.

Common Hormone Myths Debunked

- **Myth: Hormone Imbalance Is Inevitable With Age**
- *Truth:* While hormones naturally shift with age, severe symptoms and imbalances are not inevitable. Many age-related hormone changes can be significantly moderated through nutrition, movement, stress management, and lifestyle practices. Women worldwide experience vastly different menopausal transitions based largely on lifestyle factors.

- **Myth: Weight Gain Is Unavoidable During Perimenopause**
- *Truth:* Hormonal shifts can change body composition and fat distribution, but significant weight gain is not inevitable. Strategic protein intake, resistance training, stress management, and blood sugar regulation can maintain healthy body composition through the menopausal transition.

- **Myth: You Need Expensive Supplements To Balance Hormones**
- *Truth:* While some supplements can be helpful, the foundation of hormone balance lies in whole foods nutrition, quality sleep, appropriate movement, stress reduction, and environmental toxin avoidance. Many women achieve significant improvement through these lifestyle factors alone.

- **Myth: Hormone Testing Isn't Necessary If You Have Symptoms**
- *Truth:* Hormone symptoms can be similar across different imbalance patterns. Testing provides objective data to guide approaches and avoid ineffective treatments. Comprehensive testing helps identify the root causes rather than just addressing symptoms.

Understanding the facts about hormone health empowers informed decisions and avoids unnecessary treatments or restrictions. The 21-day reset is designed to help discover what actually works for unique biochemistry.

Special Considerations for Women with Existing Health Conditions

If existing health conditions are present, it's important to adapt the hormone reset approach accordingly. Always consult with a healthcare provider before beginning any new health program.

Thyroid Conditions

Women with hypothyroidism or Hashimoto's thyroiditis should:

- Be cautious with cruciferous vegetables (cook thoroughly and moderate intake)
- Consider additional selenium (200mcg daily) and zinc support
- Monitor energy levels closely during exercise and rest as needed
- Work with a practitioner to optimize thyroid medication if applicable
- Address gut health as a priority since it affects T4 to T3 conversion

PCOS

Women with polycystic ovary syndrome should:

- Place extra emphasis on blood sugar balance with regular protein intake
- Consider inositol supplementation (2-4g daily)
- Focus on anti-inflammatory foods and omega-3 fatty acids
- Emphasize regular movement to improve insulin sensitivity
- Be particularly mindful of environmental endocrine disruptors

Endometriosis

Women with endometriosis should:

- Emphasize anti-inflammatory nutrition even more stringently
- Consider additional support for estrogen metabolism (DIM, calcium-d-glucarate)
- Be cautious with certain phytoestrogens that may exacerbate symptoms
- Modify exercise during flares to focus on gentle movement
- Place extra emphasis on stress reduction techniques

Autoimmune Conditions

Women with autoimmune disorders should:

- Consider a more gradual introduction to the nutritional protocol
- Emphasize gut healing as a primary focus
- Be vigilant about tracking symptoms to identify triggers
- Modify exercise to avoid triggering flares
- Consider working with a functional medicine practitioner for personalized guidance

The 21-day reset provides a foundation that can be modified to accommodate specific health needs. The principles remain the same, but implementation may need adjustment based on individual situations.

Advanced Strategies for Persistent Hormone Imbalances

If the 21-day reset has been completed but significant hormone-related symptoms persist, consider these advanced strategies under the guidance of a healthcare practitioner.

Comprehensive Testing

Move beyond basic hormone panels to investigate:

- Heavy metal toxicity testing
- Comprehensive organic acids testing
- Genetic testing for key SNPs affecting hormone metabolism
- Advanced gut microbiome analysis
- Food sensitivity testing

Targeted Therapeutic Protocols

Based on testing results, consider specialized approaches:

- Personalized detoxification protocols for specific toxin burdens
- Tailored supplementation based on genetic methylation patterns
- Therapeutic elimination diets to identify hidden inflammatory triggers
- Specific gut healing protocols for identified pathogens or permeability issues
- Hormone precursor support based on metabolic pathway analysis

Integrative Therapies

Explore additional modalities that support hormone balance:

- Acupuncture for improving energy flow and reducing inflammation
- Specialized massage techniques like lymphatic drainage or abdominal massage
- Red light therapy for mitochondrial support and inflammation reduction
- Guided trauma release work if emotional factors are contributing
- Specialized movement practices like Feldenkrais or myofascial release

For personalized guidance on these advanced strategies, consider scheduling a consultation with a functional hormone specialist who can help develop a comprehensive plan tailored to specific needs.

The Hormone-Brain Connection: Supporting Cognitive Health

Many women experience "brain fog," memory issues, or mood changes related to hormone fluctuations. Understanding the hormone-brain connection can help support cognitive health during the reset and beyond.

How Hormones Affect the Brain

- Estrogen: Supports neurotransmitter production, protects brain cells, and promotes neural connectivity. Fluctuations can affect memory, verbal skills, and mood.
- Progesterone: Has calming effects on the brain through GABA receptors and supports myelin production. Low levels can contribute to anxiety and sleep disturbances.
- Thyroid Hormones: Regulate brain energy metabolism and neurotransmitter activity. Imbalances can cause cognitive slowing, depression, or anxiety.
- Cortisol: Acute increases support alertness, but chronic elevation damages the hippocampus (memory center) and disrupts executive function.
- Insulin: The brain relies heavily on glucose regulation. Insulin resistance can impair cognitive function and increase neuroinflammation.

Brain-Supporting Reset Strategies

- Omega-3 Fatty Acids: Prioritize fatty fish, walnuts, flaxseeds, and algae for essential brain-building fats
- Antioxidant-Rich Foods: Colorful berries, dark chocolate, and green tea protect against oxidative stress

- Blood Sugar Stability: Regular protein intake and complex carbohydrates support consistent brain energy
- Quality Sleep: Prioritize deep sleep which allows for glymphatic system cleaning of brain waste
- Stress Management: Daily mindfulness practices protect the hippocampus from cortisol damage
- Mental Stimulation: Learning new skills creates cognitive reserve and neural plasticity

Many women report significant improvements in mental clarity and emotional stability by the second week of the reset as inflammation decreases and hormone balance improves.

Hormone Balance Through the Seasons

Nature operates in cycles, and the body is designed to shift with the seasons. Adapting hormone support strategies seasonally can enhance results and align with the body's natural rhythms.

Spring (March-May)

Focus: Gentle detoxification and renewal

- Emphasize bitter greens and sprouts to support liver function
- Gradually increase movement intensity as energy rises
- Spend more time outdoors as light increases to reset circadian rhythms
- Focus on clearing stagnation through lymphatic support

Summer (June-August)

Focus: Expansion and expression

- Incorporate cooling foods like cucumber, watermelon, and mint
- Adjust workout timing to cooler morning or evening hours
- Harness peak energy for more active pursuits and social connection
- Protect sleep with blackout curtains during longer daylight hours

Autumn (September-November)

Focus: Grounding and immune strengthening

- Transition to more cooked foods and warming spices
- Incorporate immune-supporting mushrooms and herbs
- Establish consistent sleep routines as darkness increases
- Practice boundary-setting and saying "no" to preserve energy

Winter (December-February)

Focus: Rest and restoration

- Emphasize nutrient-dense, warming foods like soups and stews
- Shift toward more restorative movement practices
- Increase vitamin D supplementation and light therapy if needed
- Honor the natural inclination toward more rest and reflection

Seasonal adjustments don't require a complete overhaul of the hormone support plan, small shifts in alignment with natural cycles can yield significant benefits. Consider scheduling a mini-reset at each seasonal transition to realign hormone balance practices.

The Importance of Liver Support for Hormone Balance

The liver plays a crucial role in hormone balance by processing and eliminating used hormones. When liver function is compromised, hormones can recirculate in the body, contributing to imbalances like estrogen dominance.

Signs the Liver Needs Support

- Worsening PMS or perimenopausal symptoms
- Skin issues like acne, rashes, or excessive dryness
- Digestive complaints including bloating or nausea
- Heightened sensitivity to fragrances or chemicals
- Fatigue that worsens in the afternoon
- Waking between 1-3am (liver time in Traditional Chinese Medicine)
- Difficulty losing weight despite diet changes

21-Day Reset Liver Support Strategies

The reset incorporates specific liver support practices throughout the 21 days:

- Days 1-7: Focus on reducing liver burden by eliminating alcohol, processed foods, and excess sugar
- Days 8-14: Introduce specific liver-supporting foods like beets, artichokes, and cruciferous vegetables
- Days 15-21: Add targeted practices like castor oil packs, dry brushing, and liver-supporting herbs

Liver-Supporting Superfoods: Incorporate these powerful foods during the reset: dandelion greens, milk thistle tea, beets, artichokes, lemons, turmeric, cruciferous vegetables, and high-quality protein to provide amino acids for detoxification pathways.

Hormone-Balancing Herbs and Adaptogens

Herbal support can enhance the 21-day reset results by providing targeted assistance for specific hormone imbalance patterns. Always consult with a healthcare practitioner before adding herbs, especially if taking medications.

Ashwagandha

Primary Benefits: Adrenal support, cortisol regulation, thyroid support

Best For: Women with stress-driven hormone imbalances, subclinical hypothyroidism, anxiety, or fatigue

Typical Dose: 300-600mg standardized extract daily

Cautions: May increase thyroid hormone levels; use with caution if hyperthyroidism is present

Vitex (Chasteberry)

Primary Benefits: Supports progesterone production, regulates prolactin

Best For: PMS, irregular cycles, luteal phase defects, perimenopausal symptoms

Typical Dose: 160-240mg daily

Cautions: Avoid during pregnancy and with hormone-sensitive conditions

Rhodiola

Primary Benefits: Enhances stress resilience, supports energy and focus

Best For: Burnout, stress-induced fatigue, depression, brain fog

Typical Dose: 200-400mg (3% rosavins, 1% salidroside) daily

Cautions: May be stimulating; best taken in morning, avoid with bipolar disorder

Holy Basil

Primary Benefits: Balances cortisol, supports blood sugar, calms nervous system

Best For: Stress eating, anxiety, sleep disturbances, metabolic issues

Typical Dose: 300-500mg extract or 1-2 cups of tea daily

Cautions: May have mild blood-thinning effects, avoid before surgery

Maca

Primary Benefits: Supports overall hormone balance, enhances libido, boosts energy

Best For: Perimenopausal symptoms, fatigue, low libido, mood instability

Typical Dose: 1,500-3,000mg daily

Cautions: May be stimulating; start with lower doses to assess tolerance

Black Cohosh

Primary Benefits: Reduces hot flashes and night sweats

Best For: Perimenopausal and menopausal women with vasomotor symptoms

Typical Dose: 40-80mg standardized extract daily

Cautions: Monitor liver function with long-term use, not for women with hormone-sensitive conditions

Herbs can be powerful allies in the hormone balance journey, but they work best as part of a comprehensive approach that includes nutrition, movement, stress management, and appropriate rest.

Hormone-Balancing Movement: Beyond Exercise

The 21-day reset approaches movement as medicine, specific types of physical activity are prescribed to address particular hormone imbalances and support overall endocrine health.

Movement for Estrogen Balance

- High-Intensity Interval Training: Short bursts (20-30 seconds) of intense activity followed by longer recovery periods help metabolize excess estrogen
- Lymphatic Movement: Rebounding, dry brushing, and gentle yoga twists support elimination of estrogen metabolites
- Heat-Generating Practices: Dynamic yoga flows and moderate cardio can support healthy perspiration for detoxification

Movement for Thyroid Support

- Neck-Focused Mobility: Gentle neck stretches and shoulder opening exercises improve circulation to the thyroid
- Low-Impact Cardio: Walking, swimming, and cycling maintain fitness without stressing an already taxed system
- Strength Training: Focused resistance work supports metabolism without excessive cortisol production

Movement for Cortisol Balance

- Restorative Yoga: Supported postures activate the parasympathetic nervous system
- Tai Chi and Qigong: Flowing movements combined with breath work reduce cortisol and improve energy flow
- Nature Walking: The combination of gentle movement and natural settings has been shown to significantly lower cortisol levels

Movement for Insulin Sensitivity

- Resistance Training: Building muscle improves glucose utilization and insulin sensitivity
- Post-Meal Walking: Even 10 minutes of walking after meals significantly improves blood sugar regulation
- Interval Training: Strategic high-intensity work improves insulin receptor sensitivity

During the 21-day reset, different movement types will be experimented with to discover which provide the greatest benefit for unique hormone patterns. The goal is to develop a personalized movement prescription that supports specific needs.

Empowering Your Relationship with Healthcare Providers

Navigating the healthcare system with hormone concerns can be challenging. Many women feel dismissed or misunderstood when seeking help for hormone-related symptoms. The 21-day reset encourages becoming a health advocate and working effectively with medical professionals.

Preparing for Appointments

- Bring the symptom tracker with at least 30 days of data to show patterns
- Create a concise timeline of symptom development and interventions tried
- Prepare a prioritized list of questions (most important first)
- Research specific tests to discuss
- Bring a support person if helpful for advocating or taking notes

Effective Communication Strategies

- Use concrete, specific language rather than vague descriptions

- Describe functional impacts: "My fatigue prevents me from..." rather than just "I'm tired"
- Ask for clarification when terminology is unclear
- Express preferences clearly: "I'd prefer to try lifestyle approaches first"
- Summarize understanding before leaving: "So what I'm hearing is"

Finding the Right Practitioners

- Research providers who specialize in women's hormones and functional medicine

- Ask about their approach to testing and treatment before booking
- Consider a team approach: conventional physician, naturopathic doctor, health coach
- Trust intuition, the right provider should make you feel heard and respected
- Don't hesitate to seek a second opinion for complex hormone issues

For personalized guidance on finding healthcare practitioners for specific hormone concerns, consider scheduling a consultation with a functional hormone specialist who can provide referrals and assist in navigating options.

Extended Benefits: Beyond Hormone Balance

The 21-day hormone reset delivers benefits that extend far beyond normalized hormone levels. As the endocrine system rebalances, improvements in many aspects of health and well-being often become apparent.

Improved Digestive Function

The anti-inflammatory nutrition approach and gut-supporting practices in the reset significantly reduce bloating, constipation, and digestive discomfort for most participants.

Enhanced Skin Clarity

As inflammation decreases and detoxification pathways optimize, many women experience clearer, more radiant skin with improved elasticity and reduced breakouts.

Immune System Regulation

Hormone balance plays a key role in immune function. Many participants report fewer illnesses and reduced symptoms of allergies or autoimmune conditions.

More Stable Energy

As blood sugar stabilizes and cortisol patterns normalize, the majority of women experience more consistent energy throughout the day without afternoon crashes.

Improved Sleep Quality

Most participants report falling asleep more easily, experiencing fewer night wakings, and waking feeling more refreshed within the first 10 days of the reset.

Enhanced Mental Clarity

As hormone levels balance and inflammation decreases, cognitive function improves, with many women reporting better focus, memory, and creative thinking.

These "side benefits" of hormone balance highlight the interconnected nature of the body's systems. Supporting the endocrine system simultaneously supports digestive, immune, nervous, and integumentary (skin) systems.

Troubleshooting Common Reset Challenges

Even with the best intentions, obstacles may be encountered during the 21-day reset. The following solutions address common challenges to help stay on track.

Intense Cravings During Week 1

This is normal as the body adjusts to reduced sugar and processed foods. Try these strategies:

- Increase healthy fat and protein intake to improve satiety
- Use cinnamon, vanilla, and nutmeg to naturally satisfy sweet cravings
- Try a tablespoon of apple cider vinegar in water before meals
- Ensure calories are not restricted, hunger intensifies cravings
- Practice a 10-minute distraction technique when cravings hit

Fatigue or Headaches

These common detox symptoms typically peak around days 3-5. Support the body by:

- Increasing water intake to support elimination
- Adding a pinch of high-quality salt to maintain electrolyte balance
- Taking magnesium glycinate (300-400mg) in the evening
- Reducing exercise intensity temporarily
- Ensuring adequate protein (at least 20g) at each meal

Digestive Discomfort

Changing diet can temporarily disrupt digestion. Try these adjustments:

- Gradually increase fiber intake rather than making a sudden change
- Add digestive enzymes or a tablespoon of apple cider vinegar before meals
- Incorporate more cooked versus raw vegetables initially
- Try ginger or peppermint tea to ease discomfort
- Practice mindful eating, chewing thoroughly and eating without distractions

Temporary discomfort often signals the body is making positive adjustments. However, if symptoms are severe or persist beyond a week, consult with a healthcare provider.

Success Stories: Women's Hormone Reset Transformations

"After years of debilitating PMS and perimenopausal symptoms that were affecting my career and relationships, I was desperate for solutions. Medication helped somewhat but came with side effects. The 21-day hormone reset was life-changing, not an overnight miracle, but a gradual transformation. By day 10, my energy was more consistent, and by the end of the three weeks, my hot flashes had reduced by 80%. Four months later, I'm still implementing what I learned, and my periods are more regular than they've been in years."

Samantha, 47, Marketing Executive

"As a nurse practitioner, I was skeptical about a 'reset' program, but my own thyroid issues weren't improving despite medication. I decided to try this research-backed approach, and I'm so glad I did. The food was delicious and satisfying, not at all like a 'diet', and the movement practices were gentle but effective. What surprised me most was how much the stress management techniques affected my symptoms. My sleep improved within the first week, and my persistent brain fog lifted. My latest thyroid labs show improvement in T3 conversion, and I've now recommended the program to many of my patients."

Jennifer, 42, Nurse Practitioner

"At 38, I was struggling with unexplained weight gain, fatigue, and mood swings that were affecting my ability to be present for my children. After completing the 21-day reset, not only did I lose 8 pounds without feeling deprived, but my energy became consistent enough to eliminate my afternoon coffee dependency. The most significant change was in my emotional stability, my family has noticed I'm more patient and present. The program helped me understand my hormone patterns and gave me practical tools to support my body through perimenopause and beyond."

Maya, 38, Teacher and Mother of Three

These stories represent experiences of women who committed fully to the 21-day reset protocol. Individual results vary based on starting point, consistency, and unique biochemistry.

Bringing Partners and Family Along on Your Journey

Sustainable hormone balance is easier to achieve with support from those closest to you. Here's how to involve loved ones in the 21-day reset journey.

Educating Partners About Hormone Health

- Share specific resources about hormone imbalance to help them understand the experience
- Explain how hormones affect mood, energy, and physical well-being
- Identify specific ways they can support the reset journey
- Discuss how changes might temporarily affect household routines
- Highlight how improved hormone health will benefit relationships

Consider inviting a partner to join a consultation with a hormone specialist who can answer questions and provide objective information.

Family-Friendly Hormone Reset Strategies

- Adapt reset recipes to be enjoyed by the whole family with optional additions for those not following the protocol
- Create a "build your own" meal system where everyone starts with the same base and adds their preferred toppings
- Involve children in age-appropriate food preparation to increase their interest in healthier options
- Frame changes positively: "These foods give us energy" rather

than focusing on restrictions

- Incorporate family movement activities like nature walks, dance parties, or active games

Remember that hormone health journeys can positively influence an entire family's well-being. Modeling balanced eating, appropriate movement, and stress management teaches valuable lifelong health skills.

The Environmental Impact on Hormone Health

The modern environment contains thousands of chemicals that can disrupt hormone function. These endocrine-disrupting chemicals (EDCs) can mimic, block, or interfere with natural hormones, contributing to imbalance and symptoms.

Common Hormone Disruptors in Daily Life

- Plastics: BPA, BPS, and phthalates leach into food and water, particularly when heated
- Personal Care Products: Parabens, phthalates, and synthetic fragrances in cosmetics, lotions, and perfumes
- Household Cleaners: Synthetic fragrance, glycol ethers, and quaternary ammonium compounds
- Pesticides: Residues on conventional produce, particularly the "Dirty Dozen"
- Food Packaging: PFAS in food wrappers, microwave popcorn bags, and takeout containers
- Tap Water: Residual pharmaceuticals, pesticides, and industrial chemicals

21-Day Reset Environmental Detox Strategy

During the reset, implement these changes gradually to reduce toxic burden:

- Week 1: Replace plastic food storage with glass or stainless steel; switch to filtered water
- Week 2: Transition to clean personal care products; prioritize organic for the "Dirty Dozen" produce
- Week 3: Introduce non-toxic cleaning alternatives; evaluate household air quality

These changes support the body's natural detoxification processes and prevent additional hormone disruption during the reset period.

While it's impossible to eliminate all environmental hormone disruptors, strategic reductions can significantly decrease the overall toxic burden and support hormone balance efforts.

Meet Your Guide: Brittany Leckner

Brittany Leckner brings over a decade of experience in women's hormone health and functional wellness to the 21-Day Hormone Reset Challenge.

With specialized training in female endocrinology, nutritional biochemistry, and mind-body medicine, Brittany has helped thousands of women restore hormonal balance and reclaim vitality through evidence-based, holistic approaches.

Brittany's journey into hormone health began with her own struggles with hormonal imbalance, which conventional medicine couldn't fully address. This personal experience fueled her passion for creating accessible, effective solutions for women navigating similar challenges.

"What sets this approach apart is the integration of cutting-edge research with practical, sustainable lifestyle changes," says Brittany. "The program meets women where they are and provides the tools, support, and education needed to become active participants in their hormone health journey."

As a sought-after speaker and educator, Brittany is dedicated to empowering women with the knowledge to make informed decisions about health and well-being at every stage of life.

"The journey to hormone balance is not about perfection, it's about creating a loving relationship with your body and honoring its wisdom at every stage of life."

Brittany Leckner

Sacred Solutions Consulting: Transforming Wellness Through Integration

Sacred Solutions Consulting represents the professional services arm of Brittany Leckner's work, focused on bringing integrated hormone health approaches to healthcare systems, corporations, and wellness organizations.

Core Services

Professional Training

Educating healthcare providers on integrative approaches to women's hormone health through certification programs, workshops, and clinical mentorship.

Corporate Wellness

Designing hormone-aware workplace wellness programs that address the unique needs of women in professional environments, improving productivity and reducing absenteeism.

Healthcare Integration

Collaborating with medical practices and wellness centers to develop protocols that bridge conventional and holistic approaches to women's endocrine health.

Research Initiatives

Partnering with academic institutions to study the effectiveness of integrative approaches to hormone health and contribute to the evolving scientific understanding.

The Philosophy

Sacred Solutions Consulting is guided by the belief that true healthcare transformation happens when:

- Women's unique physiological needs are recognized and honored
- Practitioners from different disciplines collaborate rather than compete
- Evidence-based approaches from both conventional and traditional systems are integrated
- Patients become empowered participants in their health journey
- Prevention and optimization receive as much attention as disease treatment

This philosophy has positioned Sacred Solutions Consulting as a trusted advisor to healthcare organizations seeking to better serve women's health needs and improve outcomes for hormone-related conditions.

Through Sacred Solutions Consulting, Brittany Leckner works to create systemic change in how hormone health is addressed, moving beyond symptom management to true hormone optimization and whole-person wellness.

Future Innovations in Hormone Health

Looking ahead, exciting developments in hormone health research and technology promise to further enhance the ability to support women through hormonal transitions. Here's a glimpse of what's on the horizon.

Personalized Hormone Protocols

Advancements in genetic testing and metabolomics are enabling truly personalized hormone support strategies based on an individual's unique genetic predispositions and metabolic patterns. This precision approach will optimize results while minimizing unwanted effects.

Wearable Hormone Monitoring

Non-invasive wearable technology for continuous hormone monitoring is in development, allowing women to track fluctuations in real-time and adjust lifestyle factors accordingly. These devices will provide unprecedented insights into individual hormone patterns.

Microbiome-Based Interventions

Emerging research on the gut-hormone connection is leading to targeted probiotic and prebiotic formulations designed specifically to support estrobolome health and optimize hormone metabolism through the microbiome.

Advanced Phytotherapy

Sophisticated plant-based compounds that modulate hormone receptors without side effects are being developed, offering more targeted support than traditional herbal approaches while maintaining the safety profile of natural interventions.

The commitment is to bridge ancient wisdom with cutting-edge science, providing women with the most effective approaches to hormone health at every life stage.

The Ripple Effect: How Your Hormone Journey Impacts Others

Committing to hormone health creates benefits that extend far beyond personal wellbeing. This journey creates powerful ripples that positively impact relationships, community, and even future generations.

Family & Relationship Benefits

- Emotional Presence: Balanced hormones support emotional regulation, allowing for more presence and responsiveness in relationships
- Energy for Connection: Improved vitality means more capacity for meaningful engagement with loved ones
- Modeling Health: Healthy choices influence family eating patterns and stress management habits
- Reduced Tension: As mood swings and irritability decrease, household harmony typically increases
- Intergenerational Impact: Hormone health practices can influence children's future hormonal wellbeing

Community & Cultural Influence

- Breaking Taboos: Open discussions about hormone health help destigmatize women's health concerns
- Supporting Others: Personal experiences become resources for other women navigating similar challenges
- Workplace Impact: Improved focus and energy can transform professional environments and leadership
- Healthcare Advocacy: Informed patients drive positive changes in how hormone health is addressed in clinical settings
- Collective Wisdom: Sharing journeys contributes to the growing body of women's health knowledge

Prioritizing hormone health improves life and contributes to a larger movement that validates women's experiences and transforms how hormone health is understood and supported across generations.

Your Invitation to Continue the Journey

As the 21-Day Hormone Reset Challenge concludes, this is not an ending but a beginning, the first step in an ongoing journey toward sustainable hormone health and vibrant wellbeing.

Schedule Your Reset Completion Celebration

Set aside time to acknowledge commitment and progress. Review journal entries from day 1 to day 21, noting changes experienced and insights gained. This reflection reinforces achievements and helps solidify new habits.

Create Your Long-Term Hormone Support Plan

Based on the reset experience, develop a personalized maintenance plan incorporating elements that provided the greatest benefit for unique biochemistry. Include strategies for navigating challenges like travel, high-stress periods, and seasonal transitions.

Schedule Follow-Up Assessments

Plan to reassess hormone health at 3, 6, and 12 months post-reset. This might include symptom tracking, lab testing, or consultations with healthcare providers. Regular check-ins help adjust the approach as the body and life circumstances evolve.

Connect with the Community

Join an online community of women supporting each other through hormone health journeys. Share experiences, ask questions, and celebrate victories together. This ongoing connection provides motivation, accountability, and collective wisdom.

Schedule a Personal Consultation

For personalized guidance on next steps, consider booking a one-on-one consultation with Brittany Leckner or another specialist. These sessions provide targeted recommendations based on specific hormone patterns, health history, and lifestyle.

A Final Note: Your Hormone Wisdom

Dear hormone health seeker,

As this 21-day journey concludes, perhaps the most important insight is that the deepest wisdom about hormonal health already resides within.

Over these 21 days, capacity to listen to the body's signals, interpret messages, and respond with appropriate support has been developing. This communication between mind and body is the foundation of lasting hormone balance, far more powerful than any supplement, diet plan, or exercise routine.

The body constantly communicates through sensations, energy levels, emotional states, and physical symptoms. These are meaningful data, guiding toward what supports unique biochemistry and away from what disrupts it. The practices in this reset help recognize and interpret this language more clearly.

Moving forward, maintain this dialogue with the body. Notice how foods, movement patterns, relationships, and environments affect energy, mood, and physical wellbeing. Honor these observations without judgment, allowing awareness to guide choices.

Remember that hormone balance isn't a destination but a dynamic process, a dance that changes with the seasons of life. There will be times when more support is needed and times when the body functions harmoniously with minimal intervention. This rhythm is natural and to be expected.

Trust that the tools, knowledge, and awareness to navigate these changes with confidence are now in place. Each individual is the expert on their experience, the keeper of their body's wisdom, and the author of their health story.

It has been an honor to provide guidance through this transformation. The hope is to hear how the journey continues to unfold and to witness the ripple effects of renewed vitality in the world.

To enduring health and wisdom,

Brittany Leckner

"The journey to hormone balance is not about perfection, it's about creating a loving relationship with your body and honoring its wisdom at every stage of life."

About the Author

Brittany Leckner

Brittany Leckner is a wellness consultant, nutrition consultant, and integrative health advocate with a passion for helping men and women take ownership of their health journeys. With years of experience in functional medicine, men's health, women's hormone optimization, mental health, and environmental wellness, she combines evidence-based strategies with practical lifestyle approaches to create solutions that are both effective and empowering.

Her work focuses on simplifying complex health topics, whether it's balancing hormones, supporting gut health, reducing inflammation, or creating a cleaner home environment. Brittany's mission is simple: educate, empower, and elevate individuals so they can reclaim their energy, confidence, and well-being.

She is known for her no-nonsense, heart-centered approach, giving women, parents, and men the tools they need to feel supported, informed, and capable of long-term transformation.